LEVEL 3

W0099565

P.R. and Prejudice

Ann Gianola

Richmond READERS

Richmond READERS

LEVEL 1

(500 headwords)

Maria's Dilemma
Oscar
Jack's Game
The Boy from Yesterday
The Black Mountain

LEVEL 2

(800 headwords)

Jason Causes Chaos
Craigen Castle Mystery
The Road through the Hills and othes stories
Where's Mauriac?
Saturday Storm

LEVEL 3

(1200 headwords)

A Trip to the Stars
Dr Jekyll and Mr Hyde
The Canterville Ghost and Other Stories
Cold Feet
Frankenstein

LEVEL 4

(1800 headwords)

A Trip to London
Dracula   Jane Eyre
The Adventures of Tom Sawyer
Sense and Sensibility
William and Kate: A Royal Romance
A Floral Arrangement
Medical Match

LEVEL 5

(2600+ headwords)

Steve Jobs: the man behind Apple
Elizabeth II: The Diamond Queen
Sherlock Holmes & the Oxford murders

Contents

Chapter 1

A Sad Farewell

Marie took off her red apron and folded it neatly. Her last shift at *Vito's* Italian restaurant had just ended. Now she needed to return the apron to Mrs. Bertoli, the restaurant owner. Marie didn't want to say good-bye to Mrs. Bertoli, or to anyone else. After six and a half years, her co-workers at *Vito's* were more like family members. Her relationship with Mrs. Bertoli, in particular, was very special. Mrs. Bertoli had given Marie this job. She had given her a flexible schedule. And, most importantly, she had given Marie a lot of emotional support. She had encouraged Marie to stay in college even though, at times, the work was overwhelming*.

Vito's had been closed for nearly thirty minutes. It was strange that Marie suddenly couldn't find Mrs. Bertoli—or any of her co-workers. The dining room was empty. No one was at the cashier's station. She looked into the kitchen and didn't see anyone there. Finally, Marie walked into the separate banquet room that was used for private parties. "SURPRISE!" everyone shouted. Marie put one hand over her mouth and the other over her heart. She was, indeed, very surprised. Mrs. Bertoli and twenty other restaurant employees—cooks, hosts, cashiers, servers, bussers*, and dishwashers—were all waiting for her. There was a long table full of pizzas, pastas, salads, and a beautiful cake that read: *Good Luck, Marie. We'll Miss You!*

Marie tried not to cry. For a moment, she stood and stared at her dear friends. Then she walked toward the group and hugged each person. When she got to Mrs. Bertoli, she couldn't stop the tears.

"Thank you!" said Marie in a shaky voice. "You were so thoughtful to do this."

"Oh, Marie," said Mrs. Bertoli, with a wave of her hand. "It's just a little party. You're moving on to bigger and better things. And we must celebrate!" Then she signaled for Alonzo, one of the dishwashers, to turn on the Italian music. "And it's a proud day for me, too," added Mrs. Bertoli, pushing Marie toward the food. "After all, I think of you as my own child," she said, her voice also cracking with emotion. "After raising three sons, it was a blessing to have a *daughter* in my life."

Marie felt a lump in her throat. This job had been a blessing for her, too. Still, taking orders at *Vito's* was not her lifelong dream. She wanted to use her hard-earned college degree in a *real* job. Four weeks ago, she had an interview for a position at a large PR (Public Relations) firm. Two weeks ago, she had a second interview. Then, one week ago, she was offered a job as an Assistant PR Coordinator. It was just an entry-level position*. And there would be a lot of clerical* work. But there were opportunities for advancement. Marie felt happy—and very lucky.

Of course, Marie would never forget her friends at *Vito's*: Mrs. Bertoli, Alonzo, Gina, Carlo, Donna, Joey, and the rest of them. She sat down and enjoyed some delicious mushroom and black olive pizza, spaghetti with marinara sauce, and antipasto salad. Then she and her co-workers posed for pictures next to her favorite mural of Venice. Marie had always loved this painting on the wall. She especially liked the little red boat, among all the others, on the Grand Canal. Suddenly, Marie thought about the red apron draped over the back of her chair. "Oh, this is yours," she said to Mrs. Bertoli.

"You keep it," said Mrs. Bertoli. "Wear it in your kitchen."

"Thank you!" said Marie. "I'll treasure it. But I don't think I'll be cooking very much. When I need a good meal, I'll come here."

"Good. And soon, you can meet Tommaso—Tom—my youngest son. He's going to work here part-time."

"Really?" asked Marie.

"Yes. And I'm so relieved. I'm getting too old for the pressure," Mrs. Bertoli said. "When a customer complains about the seafood linguine, I want to pour it onto his head." Marie laughed.

"Then I'm very glad Tom can help you," she said, putting a hand on Mrs. Bertoli's shoulder.

"Yes, I'm losing a daughter," said Mrs. Bertoli, "but I'm getting my son back. He also has some nice ideas about improving this place. You know, he's been in the construction business for several years."

"Well," said Marie, "I look forward to meeting him. But don't let him paint over this mural. It won't be *Vito's* without it."

Mrs. Bertoli looked wistfully* at the painting. "Don't worry, Marie," she said. "I love this mural too. Venice is safe."

"And if I don't like the seafood linguine…" said Marie, protectively covering her head with both hands.

"Then don't tell me," said Mrs. Bertoli, laughing loudly. "Tell Tom."

Chapter 2

Bigger and Better Things

Marie's new job was located in a tall office building downtown. As the elevator went up, she nervously checked to see if her red apron was tied. This old habit made her smile. The red apron was in a drawer at home, of course. She was not a server at *Vito's* anymore. Marie looked in the mirror inside the elevator. She almost didn't recognize herself. She was dressed in a white lace top, a navy blue skirt, and a matching jacket. Her pretty blonde hair fell to her shoulders. She didn't have a pizza in her hands, she had a briefcase. She was living in a whole new world.

Marie was living in a whole new world.

On the twenty-second floor, Marie opened the glass doors with the gold lettering: *Emerson & Gables, Public Relations*. She walked inside the large office suite and found the receptionist. After a moment, Zack appeared and quickly led Marie down a long hallway. Marie remembered meeting Zack briefly at her second interview.

"Welcome aboard," he said, flashing his dazzlingly white smile. Then he opened a door into a meeting room. Seven other people were sitting around a table. "Everyone," said Zack quickly, "this is Marie Durand." Before Marie could say a single word, Zack continued, "And, Marie, this is our team. Anyway, you should probably sit down and take some notes."

"Thank you," said Marie, taking an empty seat at the table. Immediately, she unzipped her briefcase and took out a notebook.

"Marie, as an Assistant PR Coordinator, you're not actually *on* this team. However, we need you to support the team in every way possible. Is that clear?"

"Yes, of course," Marie replied. And for the next hour and a half, she took pages and pages of notes. Zack, the team leader, and the others had many tasks for her to do: research businesses, compile* data, make phone calls, send out and respond to e-mails, run errands, set up for meetings, and dozens of other activities. Naturally, Marie had a lot of questions. But Zack told her that Ellen, another assistant, would answer them. At the end of the meeting, Zack buttoned the jacket of his expensive suit and sped out of the room. The others quickly followed. Marie gathered up her papers and went to find Ellen.

Marie knew that the first day of any job was difficult. She tried not to look completely confused as she wandered around, reading the nameplates on the many desks and doors. *Where* was Ellen? Fortunately, Ellen soon found her.

"You must be Marie Durand," she said, shaking Marie's hand. "I'm Ellen Jenkins. I'm also an Assistant PR Coordinator, but I work for another team."

"Nice to meet you, Ellen," said Marie. "Sorry. I'm a bit lost."

"Yes, it's confusing here sometimes," said Ellen with a sigh. "But I'll show you around."

Ellen led Marie around *Emerson & Gables*, pointing out various meeting rooms, private offices, and other workspaces. There was a lovely view from all of them. Finally, she took Marie to a windowless room divided into eight cubicles. "And here is where we work," said Ellen, making an effort to smile. "Not much to see, sadly. But you'll get used to it." Then she pointed to an empty cubicle next to the wall. Marie walked toward it. "Yes, that one is yours. Feel free to add some personal touches: a plant—if you can remember to water it—and some pictures. Make yourself at home. Oh, and I've just put in a call to the IT* department. They'll be sending Ahmed to assist you with the new computer programs. He'll be over in a few minutes."

"Thanks," said Marie, pulling out the chair. "I really appreciate your help."

"You're very welcome," said Ellen kindly. "I'll come back later. In the meantime, I'm sitting right over there," she added, pointing to a cubicle on the other side of the room.

Marie sat down and looked at the computer and phone on the desk. She put down her pages of notes and looked at the blank, gray walls around her. This place was depressing. No view. No mural of the Grand Canal. *Vito's* was quite charming in comparison. For just a moment, Marie closed her eyes. She felt completely miserable. "Okay," she said to herself sternly, opening her eyes again. "You have a foot in the business world—where you've always wanted to be. You're obviously not the CEO of this company. But try and do your best." Marie reached into her briefcase and took out her pen and notepad. Then she wrote down two things to remember: *1. Think happy thoughts. 2. Find a pretty picture of Venice.*

Chapter 3

That's Not My Job!

Marie worked very hard at *Emerson & Gables*. She arrived early. She stayed late. She did everything she was asked to do—and did it well. Her reviews from Zack, his team members, and her other co-workers were all positive. At the end of ninety days, her probationary period* was over. Marie was a permanent employee and an asset to the company. She was relieved to hear it. After all, her work experience was rather limited. It was a miracle that she had been given this opportunity.

One evening after work, Marie visited an art store and bought a small print of the Grand Canal in Venice. It was by Canaletto, an eighteenth–century Italian painter. Of course, it was very different from the amateurish* mural in the banquet room that Mrs. Bertoli's late husband, Vito, had painted years ago. Although Marie appreciated both pictures, she could bring only Canaletto's version to work. The lovely image and a little African violet that survived under fluorescent lights—and without a lot of water—improved her cubicle greatly.

There were some good things about Marie's job. She loved making suggestions at meetings and working at events. The 50th anniversary celebration for the Charles Hotel was very exciting. It had taken place the previous Friday, and Zack's PR team did everything. They made announcements through social media, newspapers, television and radio. They issued party invitations to all of the VIPs. And they managed other details, like the food, music, and décor. Marie did a lot of work for the event. She wrote press releases and helped with radio ads. She even set up dozens of gold balloons in the reception area. That night, while Zack was socializing, Marie was running here and there, making sure that everything went according to schedule. The party was a huge success, and *Emerson & Gables* had another satisfied client.

Some parts of Marie's job, however, weren't quite as interesting. Too much time in the cubicle was never good. Also, Zack told her to do things that were definitely not in her job description. He frequently had Marie do personal favors for him. He had her pick up his dry cleaning. He told her to make his dental appointments. Once, he even had her book a weekend golf date. "No, it wasn't with a client," he admitted. "I'm playing with some old college buddies*. I just have to de-stress." Although Marie felt annoyed by these tasks, she tried not to show it.

Yesterday, Zack had given Marie another ridiculous chore. It was 6:00p.m. and she was just leaving the office. Suddenly, Zack appeared at her cubicle. "You need to pick up some Chinese take-out food for two," he said. "And a nice bottle of white wine," he added, handing her the company credit card. Marie had a feeling that this also wasn't business-related. This errand would take another forty-five minutes of her time. She felt more like a waitress than an Associate PR Coordinator.

"Here," Zack said, giving her the address of the restaurant. "You'll save me a lot of time. I don't want to stop on my way home."

In spite of Zack's arrogance, there was something fascinating about him. He was very tall and good-looking, with light brown hair and piercing blue eyes. He had a $200 hairstyle (Marie made those appointments, too) and designer clothes. His teeth were incredibly white—probably due to his regular dental visits. More than anything, Marie was curious how this man had come so far in his career. Zack was only four or five years older than she was, and yet he was the picture of success. Marie also hoped to be successful someday, but she would *never* spend $200 on a hairstyle or send some underling* to pick up her dinner.

Zack was definitely taking advantage of Marie. She wanted to say, "Hey, I have a life too. And it's time for me to go home." Instead, she readily agreed to help him. Zack was in a powerful position. He could promote* her in the future. Marie could be *on* the team instead of just supporting it. She wanted to be out of the dreary cubicle and into a bright outer office. Therefore, she politely nodded. Then she used the same words she had said countless times at *Vito's*: "Sure. What can I get for you?"

Chapter 4

An Unwelcome Invitation

Marie's new job consumed most of her time and energy. She had been to *Vito's* only a few times since she left six months ago. A week after her going-away party, she brought her former co-workers a thank-you card and a big basket of food: smoked salmon, fruit, assorted cheeses, crackers, nuts, and a delicious lemon cake. Then, two months later, she went in one night for dinner. Unfortunately, Mrs. Bertoli wasn't there, and everyone else was very busy. Marie ordered from the to-go menu and paid a cashier who she had never met. Her third visit was just last Saturday. In the early afternoon, she went to a bridal shower for Gina in the banquet room.

Marie was very glad to receive an invitation. She was delighted for Gina and her fiancé, Dominic. They were a sweet couple, and would undoubtedly live happily ever after. It was wonderful to see Mrs. Bertoli and many of her old friends again. Marie made small talk with everyone: "The new job is great, thank you. Yes, it's really exciting to be downtown." On the outside, Marie was smiling. Inside, however, she had begun to feel very sad—almost on the verge* of tears.

Marie felt unhappy for a reason: she didn't belong at *Vito's* anymore. Her time card wasn't in the back office. No one needed her to carry a large pizza into the dining room. She couldn't joke with Alonzo and Carlo in the kitchen. This stage of her life was over. These relationships, even the one with Mrs. Bertoli, felt different now. Mrs. Bertoli had hired another college student—probably the new cashier—and taken her under her wing. Soon, no one would remember her.

Sometimes, Marie felt very insecure*. She hadn't had a very stable childhood. Her mother died of *complications* when she was about seven. Her father didn't explain exactly what that meant, and Marie found it too painful to ask. Then, shortly after her nineteenth birthday, Marie's father also died of *complications*—or what she now understood to be the effects of alcoholism. He left her a little money, but certainly not enough for rent and college tuition. She had to work. And that's when, like a stray cat, Marie wandered into *Vito's* to ask for a job. Mrs. Bertoli liked her—or perhaps felt sorry for her. Nevertheless, Marie was a very good worker. And, in time, Mrs. Bertoli became her surrogate* parent.

Marie bit her lower lip. This sadness wasn't useful. Marie had chosen to leave *Vito's* and follow her dreams of becoming a professional. And she'd gotten what she'd always wanted: a job in PR. Well, she'd never dreamed about the dullness of the gray cubicle or running out for Zack's Chinese food. But, in truth, she had come a long way from that nineteen-year-old stray cat. She had succeeded with the help of some kind-hearted people, like Mrs. Bertoli. But things didn't always stay the same. People grew apart. Life went on at *Vito's* and everywhere else.

As Gina unwrapped fluffy new towels and sparkling glassware, Marie looked over at her favorite mural. As usual, she focused on the little red boat, among all the others, on the Grand Canal. "I need to concentrate on my own journey," she thought, "and not let my insecurities get me down." Suddenly, she heard a voice behind her. It was Mrs. Bertoli's.

"I forgive you for not visiting me regularly," she whispered. "Of course, you had to get used to your new career." Marie turned around and smiled. "And we've been busy here too, I'll admit. There have been a lot of changes since my son came. But I haven't forgotten you," said Mrs. Bertoli, squeezing Marie's hand.

"Oh," said Marie, "please don't worry about that." Still, she felt comforted by Mrs. Bertoli's kind words. "We're both busy. But I hope it's not too long before we see each other again."

"It won't be," said Mrs. Bertoli matter-of-factly. "You're coming to my house for dinner a week from tomorrow. You must meet Tom. I've been thinking about this for a long time," she continued. "I *know* the two of you will hit it off. You're not seeing anyone, are you?"

"Well, no," said Marie, her face changing to the color of the little red boat. "Um, thanks. I'll check my calendar…"

Mrs. Bertoli laughed and waved her hand. "There's nothing important on your calendar," she persisted. "So, you'll be there next Sunday at 6:00p.m." Then Mrs. Bertoli sat back in her chair, and Marie politely admired the fluffy towels that Donna had just passed to her. Suddenly, Marie's emotions were completely different. She no longer felt like crying. She felt like running.

Chapter 5

Pride and Prejudice

Before Marie left the bridal shower at *Vito's*, she peeked*
into the kitchen. She saw Joey arranging slices of pepperoni
on a pizza. She saw Alonzo carrying a stack of clean dishes.
And, from behind, she saw another man. He was bent
over a saucepot. He had a red apron and a white chef's hat
with longish, gray hair sticking out the bottom of it. Well,
perhaps the gray was from flour rather than age. Flour got
everywhere in the kitchen. Anyway, Marie supposed that he
was Tom, and her first impression—based on a two-second
glance—was not great. She turned away quickly and left
through the front door.

Marie walked toward the bus stop, kicking a little rock
on the sidewalk. She'd felt both happiness and sadness at
Vito's today. But now she felt only regret. Mrs. Bertoli had
been like a mother to her. If Marie refused to meet her son,
it could ruin their relationship forever. This left her very few
options. She could pretend to be sick. Or she could pretend
to be busy. But these were only temporary solutions. Mrs.
Bertoli would just reschedule their dinner. Perhaps she could
pretend to suddenly have a boyfriend: "Hello? Mrs. Bertoli?
Well, things have gotten more serious with someone at
work. His name is Zack. And he can be rather jealous…"

These excuses sounded phony*. Even worse, Mrs. Bertoli
would never believe them. Mrs. Bertoli had done so much
for Marie over the years. Obviously she couldn't lie to her.
There was nothing else she could do. She had to go to Mrs.
Bertoli's house next Sunday with some flowers. Then she

had to be civil—yet not encouraging—to her son while they ate dinner together. Monday was a workday, so Marie couldn't possibly stay late. It was all settled, and she must face the evening bravely.

Marie knew Mrs. Bertoli's two older sons very well. Luigi and Giuseppe went by the nicknames Lou and Joe. They ate at *Vito's* often with their wives and children. Marie was always happy to wait on them, and they used to tip her generously. They were both in their thirties and made a good living, but they were definitely among the working class. Lou was an auto mechanic, and Joe had a plumbing business. Lou and Joe were perfect examples of *salt of the earth* types: honest, decent, and unpretentious*.

Needless to say, Marie appreciated good qualities in people. And perhaps Tom was a very good person, too. However, since beginning her new job, Marie had become interested in a different *type* of man. He wasn't an auto mechanic, a plumber, or a construction worker. And he didn't wear a red apron and have flour in his hair. Instead, he wore an expensive suit and had a $200 hairstyle. He played golf and had other people pick up his dinner. He led business meetings and had piercing blue eyes. Somehow, Zack—or someone like him—was more appealing.

It was hard for Marie to admit this preference. And perhaps her prejudice against working-class men was unfair. But she wanted to distance herself from where she started in life. Finishing college and getting a real job were steps in the right direction. Dating Tom, she knew, was a step in the wrong one. Marie still had a long way to go professionally. Although Mrs. Bertoli had been like a mother, she could never be her *mother-in-law*. Marie had higher hopes for a boyfriend and future husband. She and Tom were simply an impossible match.

Marie's determination to succeed began when she was very young. Fifteen years ago, while waiting for her father in front of a liquor store, two women had stared at her as they walked by. "Poor thing," said one. "She doesn't stand a chance in life."

"Yes," said the other, "her mom was a mess. And her dad is just plain trash."

"Oh, well," said the first. "Nothing can be done for her, then. Everyone knows that *the apple doesn't fall far from the tree*." Angry tears sprang into Marie's eyes. True or not, it hurt to hear their cruel comments about her parents. But their judgment of *her* felt even worse. As the women crossed the street, Marie clenched her fists. She was *not* going to be a tragic character. She was not a hopeless case. And she would be successful—in spite of their awful prediction. Later in life, she would prove those horrible women wrong. She would prove everyone wrong.

Chapter 6

CD1

An Unpleasant Discovery

On Monday, Zack's team had a meeting. As usual, Marie joined the group to take notes. At this particular meeting, Zack had big news. They were getting a new client: Eliza Adams, the *haute couture* fashion designer. Eliza Adams had stores all over the world. And now, a store was coming to their city. Zack paced nervously around the room.

"This is huge," he said. "Eliza Adams has hired *Emerson & Gables* to do all of her PR: press conferences, media announcements, promotions, and everything else. We're even doing the grand opening of her store on 5th Avenue."

Marie felt as excited as everyone else in the room. Eliza Adams was very famous. Her clothes were all over the runway and the red carpet. They were in all the high fashion magazines. Celebrity brides—or very rich ones— wore her wedding gowns. Marie began to write furiously in her notebook. Yes, she had some ideas for this account. And it was time to work very hard, especially since she wanted a promotion. Surely she was too good to be stuck in the cubicle forever, like Ellen Jenkins.

Ellen had spent the last three and a half years in the cubicle. According to Ellen, she had received a few small salary increases but she remained just an Assistant PR Coordinator. Marie observed that she was an excellent worker, too. Ellen always trained the new employees. Marie couldn't understand why this creative, competent person hadn't been asked to join a team.

"Because they like me where I am," explained Ellen, while they ate lunch together. "I'm good at my job, but, more importantly, I make them look good."

"You have a lot of experience now," said Marie. "Have you thought about looking for another job?"

"Oh, yes," admitted Ellen, "many times. But, you know, the job market is really tough right now. And my team leader says that she'll think of me the minute something comes up." Ellen laughed and took a sip of her lemonade. "Of course, I've heard that story for over three years. In the meantime, several new people *have* joined her team. But none of them came from our department."

This news made Marie lose her appetite. She put down her sandwich.

"Not one?" she asked. "At my interview, I was told that good workers were almost always promoted."

"That's what they want us to think," said Ellen, snapping a potato chip in two. "But I've never seen it. I shouldn't tell you that, though. It isn't fair. Besides, what do I know about your team? Maybe Zack will promote you soon."

Marie's thoughts returned to the present. Zack was still pacing around the meeting room. "We need to do a lot of research on Eliza Adams," he commanded. "This is an enormous account, and we have to do everything right. And we don't have a lot of time. Her *people* are coming for a presentation in less than two weeks. We need some brilliant ideas. We must impress them."

"I have some ideas," interrupted Marie, almost without thinking. "There should be a drawing at the grand opening. The winner gets a gown from the store."

"I love that!" said Evelyn. "What a great idea!"

"And turquoise is their brand's signature color," Marie continued. "We should have Eliza Adams arrive at the grand opening in a turquoise convertible. And, at an event this size, we should have a turquoise fireworks display." Everyone in the room nodded with approval. "We'll have to have all the news stations there, of course. And the morning TV show on Channel 7 has a fashion segment. Eliza Adams must make an appearance."

"Can you hold these thoughts for a bit, Marie?" asked Zack, putting up his hand to stop her. "We're getting ahead of ourselves. I think we've discussed this enough for now. I'll call another meeting soon. I think everyone knows what to do now." Zack opened the door and waited for everyone to leave. As Marie walked toward the door, Zack said, "Can you wait a minute, Marie? I'd like to talk to you."

"Okay," she said. She thought Zack probably wanted to order his lunch.

"You had some nice ideas about the Eliza Adams account," he said, smiling brightly.

"I have more," said Marie. "I probably wrote down twenty things during our meeting. And I can easily come up with twenty more."

"In that case," said Zack, "let's discuss them over dinner. How about this Friday evening? I'll pick you up at 8:00p.m."

Chapter 7

Dinner with Zack

There were now two social events on Marie's calendar this week. The first, dinner with Zack, she looked forward to excitedly. The second, dinner with Mrs. Bertoli and Tom, she completely dreaded. Naturally, she tried to focus on the meeting with Zack. She still couldn't believe it. On Friday, she and Zack were going to discuss the Eliza Adams account. Surely this meant that Marie was ready to be *on* the team.

For the past several months, Marie had supported Zack's team in every way. Her research was thorough. Her reports were meticulous*. Her work at events was first-rate. She responded to more phone calls and e-mails than anyone else. Her skills in dealing with vendors and clients were excellent. She received wonderful reviews from Evelyn, Mateo, Silvia, and the others on the team: "Fantastic job, Marie!" "We couldn't have done this without you, Marie!" "You're the absolute best, Marie!"

Marie rightly believed that she was as smart and capable as everyone on Zack's team—including Zack. Therefore, she refused to spend an eternity in the cubicle. Unlike Ellen, she was not going to wait patiently to be promoted someday. Marie was determined to climb the corporate ladder*. She deserved more money and a better view. She also deserved more respect—and fewer lunch orders. So, Marie did what she had to do. She prepared an amazing presentation at home. Then, at dinner, she planned to impress Zack with her brilliant PR ideas for the Eliza Adams store. This was a chance to advance her career, and she was going for it.

On Friday, Marie hurried home from the office. She took a shower, carefully did her hair and makeup, and put on her favorite purple silk dress—a birthday gift from Mrs. Bertoli. After quickly reviewing the presentation, she put her laptop into her briefcase and went outside at 8:00p.m. Zack pulled up twenty minutes later, and Marie got into his car. "Hello," said Zack, without an apology for being late.

"Good evening," said Marie, attempting to smooth out her hairstyle, now somewhat ruined by standing in the wind.

"Glad you could do this," said Zack, his teeth visible even in the dark. His luxury car smelled new. For some reason, Marie thought of her father's old pickup truck, with its torn upholstery held together with duct tape. "So this is what success feels like," thought Marie, moving her hand along the smooth leather seat. "If only my dad could see me now."

Zack left his car with a *valet*, and they entered one of the finest—and most expensive—French restaurants in the city: *Les Etoiles*. Inside, the *maître d'* led Marie and Zack to a quiet booth in the corner. Soon a *sommelier* appeared to offer them some wine. This was certainly a different environment from *Vito's*, where there were definitely no *valets*, *maître d's* or *sommeliers*. Marie almost laughed to imagine her co-workers in any of these roles. Zack, however, seemed very familiar with the restaurant. "Don't worry about it," he said, reaching over and closing the menu in Marie's hands. "I'll order for both of us."

"Oh, okay," said Marie. "If you say so." She tried to believe that Zack was trying to be helpful. Her high school French was, in fact, a little rusty*. But deep inside, she knew that he was being condescending*. Zack had ways of making a person feel inferior, and this was obviously another one.

"*Garçon!*" called Zack loudly, snapping his fingers at their server. Marie was horrified. She could almost forgive Zack for not using the correct word for their server: *Monsieur*. But snapping his fingers at him—or anyone else—was completely wrong. If Mrs. Bertoli were here, his $200 hairstyle would

Marie was horrified by Zack's behavior.

be covered in seafood linguine. Nevertheless, their server appeared on command and dutifully took Zack's order for their appetizer, entrée and dessert.

Marie sadly identified with their server. Although the man politely noted their order, and endured Zack's terrible French pronunciation, she knew that he was angry and upset. Who wouldn't be? Marie had been in the server's position many times. Over the years, several customers had been very rude at *Vito's*. But no one had *ever* snapped their fingers at her. Marie offered their server an apologetic look. She wished to say, "*Monsieur*, I'm *really* sorry!" But she just couldn't. This was not the time to speak up and teach Zack better manners. In spite of his appalling* behavior, Marie stayed quiet for one reason: she wanted to join Zack's team.

Chapter 8

Marie Makes a Promise

Their French meal was delicious, and Zack, thanks to the wine, became more polite toward the staff at *Les Etoiles*. "Send my compliments to the chef," he said to their server. "Everything is *fantastique*."

He also liked Marie's ideas about the Eliza Adams account. He was delighted by the detailed presentation on her laptop. By the time they had their coffee and *crème brûlée*, Marie had chosen to forget about Zack's boorish* behavior. He didn't really look down on restaurant employees. She had just imagined that prejudice. Once again, she was under his spell.

"I'm glad you liked my presentation," said Marie, closing her laptop.

"Liked it? I *loved* it," said Zack. "And the client's representatives will too. Everyone needs to see this. I knew you were talented, Marie. But I didn't know that you were in this league." Marie blushed. This was exactly what she wanted to hear.

"Thanks, Zack. Of course, I'll share it with the team," she said, enjoying the rich aroma of her French coffee. "And…if possible…I'd really like to help during the presentation next week. Is that okay?"

Zack looked down for a moment and twisted the cloth napkin on the table.

"Definitely," he said. "No one has worked harder on this account than you have, Marie. You deserve to be there." Then he let go of the napkin and reached for Marie's hand.

"You're a valuable resource at *Emerson & Gables*," said Zack, stroking her hand tenderly. "Don't forget that. I thought you were team material. But this proves it," he said, pointing to her computer. "The presentation will be a huge hit." Marie beamed with pride, but slowly moved her hand away from Zack's, feigning* a sudden need to stir her coffee. Although Zack was very attractive, his touch felt uncomfortable.

When they had finished discussing business, Zack removed the credit card from his wallet. It was the one he used for his expenses at *Emerson & Gables*. Seeing that Marie had noticed, Zack offered an excuse: "It's business." Then Zack paid the bill and they got up to leave. As they walked through the restaurant, Zack put his arm around Marie's waist. "You look very pretty tonight, by the way," he said.

"Oh, thank you," said Marie, stepping away from him. On the drive back to her apartment, Marie continued to talk about the Eliza Adams account. Zack didn't pay much attention.

"I'm going to have a very relaxing weekend, thanks to you," said Zack. "We're ready for the client's representatives right now."

"But we're not ready, Zack," said Marie seriously. "We'll need next week to work on the presentation. And we must add other ideas from the team. But this is a good start. I'm really excited about the plans so far, too."

Zack pulled up in front of Marie's building. This time, he got out and opened Marie's door. "I had a great time tonight. You've made me very happy," he said, leaning in to hug her tightly. "I always thought that you were a beautiful woman, but I didn't know that you were so gifted in PR."

"Thanks," said Marie, freeing herself from his arms quickly. She could appreciate that Zack was both handsome and successful, but she couldn't allow things to get romantic. She worked for Zack. Luxury cars and expensive meals in restaurants were nice, but this evening needed to end. They had to see each other every day at the office. Marie didn't want to complicate things tonight.

"Shall I come up for a while?" asked Zack, looking up at her building.

"Oh," said Marie. "Sorry, not tonight. *Really* tired." She forced out a yawn. "I got almost no sleep this week— working on this," she said, looking down at her briefcase. "But we'll be in touch soon. Monday morning, right?"

"It's a deal," said Zack. "But make a promise to me right now."

"Sure," said Marie. "What is it?"

"Before you brush your teeth and turn out the lights, you must do one more thing," he said, pulling gently on one of her blonde curls.

"Yes?" asked Marie curiously.

"Send me that amazing presentation."

Chapter 9

Dinner with Tom

It was nearly 5:00p.m. on Sunday before Marie got dressed to go to Mrs. Bertoli's house. This time there was no silk dress, no fancy hairstyle, and no special makeup. She put on an old, loose-fitting gray sweater over a pair of black yoga pants. Then she pulled her hair back into a messy ponytail. Obviously it wasn't the look she'd created for dinner with Zack. But this wasn't dinner with Zack. And she certainly wasn't trying to attract Tom's attention. If he asked to see her again, she had planned exactly what to say: "Sorry, but I'm just not ready for a relationship right now. It's not you—it's me."

Marie picked up the bouquet of flowers that she had bought earlier at the market. Then she took the bus across town to Mrs. Bertoli's neighborhood. About thirty minutes later Marie got off the bus, walked four blocks, and knocked on Mrs. Bertoli's red front door. Mrs. Bertoli quickly opened it and hugged Marie warmly. "I'm so glad to see you!" she exclaimed. "Please come in and make yourself at home."

Marie stepped into the house and handed Mrs. Bertoli the flowers.

"How lovely," Mrs. Bertoli said appreciatively. "But you didn't have to do that."

"Oh, it's the least I could do. Thank you for inviting me," said Marie, "Wow! Something smells really good in here!"

"That's Tom's creation," Mrs. Bertoli boasted. "It's a vegetarian lasagna. He wants to put it on our menu at *Vito's*." Mrs. Bertoli had to laugh. "He's bringing Italian *nouvelle cuisine* to the restaurant, if you can imagine. Tom wants our food to be fresher, lighter, and healthier. I'm not sure what our old customers will think, but it does smell good." Marie followed Mrs. Bertoli into the kitchen, where Mrs. Bertoli fetched a vase from a cabinet and carried it to the sink. She added some water and put Marie's flowers inside. "Don't they look pretty!" she said.

Just then, a tall man came into the kitchen. He had wet, longish, dark brown—not gray—hair. He had gorgeous hazel eyes and a soft three-day beard. Over his jeans, he wore a wrinkled button-down shirt. His sleeves were rolled up a little, exposing his strong, olive-skinned forearms. His appearance was the opposite of Zack's. His clothes weren't expensive and his teeth were a more natural shade of white. Nevertheless, Marie had to admit that Mrs. Bertoli's son was very good-looking.

"Ah, Tommaso!" Mrs. Bertoli cried. "You must meet my dear friend, Marie. And Marie," she said, "I'd like you to meet my youngest son, Tommaso—or Tom, as he prefers to be called."

"Nice to meet you, Tom," said Marie, politely but coolly.

"Yes, you too," said Tom. Then, turning toward his mother, he said, "You didn't mention that we were having a guest for dinner." He was obviously surprised by Marie's presence—and *not* particularly happy that she was there. Marie was surprised too. *She* was supposed to feel awkward in this situation. And *he* was supposed to feel overjoyed that Marie—a beautiful, educated, and professional young woman—had come to meet him. Clearly, this was not the case at all. Of course, Marie did not want to date Tom. But his indifference toward her was a bit hard on her ego. Suddenly, she truly regretted wearing her ugly gray sweater.

"Marie isn't a guest," said Mrs. Bertoli. "She's part of the family. I've wanted the two of you to meet for a long time. She worked for several years at *Vito's*, you know."

"Hmm," said Tom, as he bent down and looked inside the glass window in the oven door. "Well, dinner won't be ready for another twenty minutes or so. Hope that's okay. You two go into the living room and talk. I'll stay in here and finish the salad."

"Nonsense!" said Mrs. Bertoli. "I finished the salad when you were in the shower. And the garlic bread is nearly ready." Tom reluctantly followed his mother and Marie into the living room and sat down. "Marie, what can I get for you?" asked Mrs. Bertoli. "Would you like a glass of wine? I also have your favorite soda, Italian grapefruit."

"The Italian soda will be fine," said Marie. "This is a work night for me."

"I can get that for her, Mom," said Tom, standing up. Marie knew that he was looking for any excuse to leave the room.

"Sit down, Tom," Mrs. Bertoli replied firmly, "and talk to Marie. She has an exciting career now. You must ask her all about it."

Chapter 10

A Hilarious Ride Home

Tom sighed loudly enough for Marie to hear him. "So, where do you work?" he asked, as Mrs. Bertoli walked into the kitchen.

"I work at *Emerson & Gables*. That's a PR firm," answered Marie, pulling at the sleeve of her baggy sweater. "That stands for public relations," she continued, somewhat haughtily*. "Perhaps you've never heard of that. Well, it means that we…manage communication between an organization and the public…in order to…"

"I know," interrupted Tom impatiently. He felt that Marie was insulting his intelligence. "I have heard of public relations. And I *know* what people in PR do." Just then, Mrs. Bertoli returned to the living room with drinks for everyone. She was the only person smiling. She didn't notice the tension between Marie and Tom at all. A very long twenty minutes later, they all went into the dining room. Marie spoke very little during their meal. She liked the lasagna. She praised Mrs. Bertoli for her organic green salad. And she completely agreed that both items should be added to the menu at *Vito's*.

Fortunately, Mrs. Bertoli liked to talk a lot. She filled the gaps in the conversation with her friendly chatter and laughter. She made Tom discuss some ideas he had for changes at *Vito's*. In addition to the healthier menu items, he planned to add an outdoor patio area. "What a great idea," said Marie, looking only at Mrs. Bertoli. "I can't wait to see that!"

A few minutes after Marie finished her rich cannoli, something clearly not on the healthy-items menu, she looked at her watch. "You will think that I'm incredibly rude. But I'm afraid that I must get going now. The buses on Sunday night don't run very often."

"So soon?" asked Mrs. Bertoli. "You just got here! And we were having such a lovely time!"

Marie couldn't possibly describe this evening the same way. Nearly every moment had been uncomfortable, and Tom seemed absolutely miserable.

"I can give you a ride," offered Tom, perhaps feeling a little guilty about his unfriendliness.

"No thanks," said Marie. "I should walk off this cannoli."

"You're getting a ride from Tom," insisted Mrs. Bertoli. "And that's final."

Since this evening probably couldn't get any worse, Marie accepted his offer. "Thank you so much for having me," she said, giving Mrs. Bertoli a hug good-bye. "I'll see you soon at *Vito's*".

"You'd better," said Mrs. Bertoli. "Keep in touch! And drive carefully, you two!"

Except for Marie's occasional directions, Tom and Marie sat silently in his hybrid* car. It was actually Tom who finally spoke. "I wasn't expecting company tonight," he said. "Sorry for being a bit antisocial."

"Please don't be," said Marie. "I thought you were delightful." She began to laugh. And she couldn't stop. Then Tom began to laugh too. "I especially appreciated your interest in my job," Marie added sarcastically*.

"Yes," said Tom. "And I liked it when you thought that I was too simple-minded to understand the PR business."

"Okay," said Marie, still laughing. "I deserved that. But please give me a break. This wasn't my idea. Your mother invited me to dinner tonight. It was obvious that you weren't happy about it."

"It wasn't my intention to hurt your feelings," Tom said earnestly. "A few weeks ago, my mother suggested inviting you over to meet me. Unfortunately, she has it in her head that I'm desperately lonely—which I'm *not*. Anyway, I told her *no* quite firmly. So I didn't think she would do it anyway. Most thirty-one-year-old men don't have their mothers find women for them, do they?"

Marie began to laugh. And she couldn't stop.

Marie had to reach into her purse for a tissue to wipe away the tears of laughter that were now streaming down her face. "It's funny now," she said. "But I wasn't thrilled about this plan either. Still, I love your mother, Tom. She has helped me so much in my life. I will be forever in her debt. When she asked me to come over and meet her son, what could I say?"

"And I see that you dressed up for the evening," Tom laughed, looking over at her outfit.

"You too," she said. "Don't you own an iron?"

"I didn't know you were coming!" Tom protested. "I was just spending Sunday evening with my mom—testing a few recipes. I didn't know that she'd brought home my bride." Now Tom also began laughing uncontrollably.

"It's all over now," said Marie, as Tom rounded the corner on to her street. "You're quite safe." She was holding her cheeks from laughing so hard. "But in case you had fallen madly in love with me, at least I had an excuse prepared." Marie cleared her throat and said: "Sorry, but I'm just not ready for a relationship right now. It's not *you*…"

"Let me finish that thought," said Tom, smiling from ear to ear. "It's *me*!"

Chapter 11

Unnecessary Errands

On Monday, Marie arrived at *Emerson & Gables* a few minutes early. She went to Zack's corner office, but he was on the phone, his feet on the desk. He flashed his dazzling smile, pointed to the phone, and signaled that he would be five more minutes. So Marie went into her dingy work area and found her cubicle. It was quite a contrast from Zack's office, with its expensive furniture and lovely view. Marie straightened her Canaletto print. Then she made sure her African violet had enough—but not too much—water.

In less than five minutes, Zack came to Marie's cubicle. He immediately handed her a very long to-do list. "I'll need you to do these things ASAP," said Zack with authority. "And this may take several hours," he added, "but it will be a nice change for you. Enjoy the fresh air and exercise."

Marie read Zack's list. There was nothing important on it. In fact, there were a few things that Marie shouldn't do at all: buy his sister a birthday present, take his dirty shirts (already in a large bag under her desk) to the laundry, and pick up a teeth-whitening kit from the pharmacy. "Oh, and it must be the pharmacy over on 63rd Street," said Zack, pointing to the list. "They carry the brand that I like." "But, Zack," said Marie, looking up at him, "there is so much we need to do here. The representatives for Eliza Adams are coming this *Friday*! We need every hour to work on the presentation. Oh," she added, "after I sent it to you last Friday, were you able to open it? I wasn't sure if you had the same operating system at home."

"Shh!" said Zack, lowering his voice. "Not so loud. Yes, it's fine. But I need you to do these things today. I'll meet with the team this morning to discuss some general stuff. Everything is under control here. Go!" he said, dragging out the laundry bag and handing it to Marie. "Get out of your cage for a while. And," he said, pulling exactly $6.00 from his wallet, "I'm buying you lunch."

Marie was astonished as she stood by the elevator, carrying the long list, her purse containing an extra $6.00, and Zack's heavy laundry bag. She didn't want to leave the office. Why was Zack sending her away? What was he thinking? There were so many important things to do! Marie sighed. Perhaps this meant that things were under control. The presentation was in excellent shape and maybe, with some minor changes, it would be ready to share this Friday. They still had several weeks to prepare for the actual events. Marie shrugged her shoulders and left the building.

◆ ◆ ◆

It was nearly 5:00p.m. when Marie returned to the office. She'd traveled all over the city. Most of what she had to do was unnecessary. She'd hand-delivered a contract to a business several miles away. Another stop had been at a Greek restaurant to order lunch for the clients on Friday. Almost everything could have been accomplished electronically or on the telephone. Nevertheless, Marie had done everything on the list, including Zack's personal errands. For lunch she'd bought a hot dog and a bottle of water, costing slightly over $6.00. Now, it was time to do something productive.

Marie stopped in Zack's office. He wasn't there, but she left two shopping bags and a receipt for his laundry on the desk. Then she went into the women's restroom to wash her hands. At the sink, she saw Evelyn.

"I haven't seen you all day," said Evelyn, drying her hands with a paper towel. "We missed you at the meeting."

"Oh," replied Marie. "Zack asked me to do a bunch of errands today. One of them was to arrange the client lunch on Friday."

"Is that so?" said Evelyn, frowning. "Well, we needed your help *here*. There's so much to do! You know, Zack is using two of your great ideas. Do you remember the drawing at the grand opening? And the turquoise fireworks display? He included them in his brilliant presentation. Gosh, I don't know when he found the time to put it together. I guess that's why he's the boss!"

"I guess so," said Marie, too shocked to say anything else.

"Anyway, we must do a lot of research before Friday. We need you here!" Evelyn said, pushing open the restroom door. "You do such a great job supporting us, Marie. We would be lost without you."

"Really?" said Marie after the door closed behind Evelyn. Now she was absolutely furious. "Good to know."

Chapter 12

Shocked and Upset

At the sink, Marie ran some water on a paper towel and put it on her forehead. She felt sick to her stomach. What was Zack doing? And why did he exclude her from the meeting today? Even worse, why didn't he give her credit for the *whole* presentation? Marie needed a few minutes to calm down. Then she went directly to Zack for some answers.

Once again, Marie found Zack on the phone, his feet on the desk. Marie stayed in the doorway, even though Zack signaled that he would be five more minutes. She refused to return to her cubicle. "Look, let me call you back, sweetheart," said Zack. "Two minutes. Promise. Yeah, you too." Then he hung up the phone and put his feet on the floor. "Hey, Marie. I found the things you bought for me. But maybe you should keep this receipt for the laundry," he said, waving the yellow paper at her. "I'll need you to pick up my clean shirts on Thursday." Marie acted like she didn't see it.

"Excuse me, Zack," said Marie, with her hands clenched in front of her. "I just ran into Evelyn. Apparently, I missed *your* brilliant presentation. Is there a reason why I wasn't at the team meeting today?" Zack's face reddened. With his contrasting white teeth, he looked like a monster.

"No, of course not. I just needed your help in other ways. Look Marie," said Zack, motioning for her to sit down. "I know you're excited about the Eliza Adams presentation. And your enthusiasm is great. But we're in this together—as a team."

"Sorry, Zack," said Marie, without sitting. "But I don't think you asked anyone else on the *team* to take your dirty shirts to the laundry."

"Listen," said Zack, now in a more serious tone. "Our common goal is to increase business at *Emerson & Gables*. It's a group effort. One person doesn't get all of the credit. You're a good Assistant PR Coordinator. And you have a lot of potential*. Someday *you* might be sitting in an office. But you don't have the experience yet. You still have a lot to learn."

"Yes," said Marie, "perhaps I do. But I'm not sure what I can learn by doing your shopping."

"Marie," said Zack, his blue eyes icy, "you look tired. Go home and get some rest." He reached for the phone and put his feet back on his desk. Marie really wanted to pour a plate of seafood linguine on his head. Instead, she walked toward the door.

"Just one more thing, Zack," she said, turning around. "You promised that I could share my ideas at the presentation on Friday. You're not changing your mind, are you?"

"Of course not, Marie! Don't worry. You will play a *major* role on Friday. I will introduce you to everyone and give you the credit that you deserve."

Marie walked out of Zack's office without taking the receipt for his laundry. She was upset about missing the team meeting. But Zack was still her boss. She couldn't be angry and uncooperative. Bad behavior could get her fired. Instead, Marie returned to her dreary work area. Her co-workers had already left their cubicles for the day. Marie went to hers and sat down. Her desk was covered in work for other people. She had dozens of voicemails and e-mails. Zack's suggestion that she "go home and get some rest" was impossible. Marie let out a loud groan.

"What was that for?" asked Ellen from the other side of the room. "Has it been one of those days?"

"Sorry!" Marie apologized, getting up and walking toward Ellen's cubicle. "I didn't mean to disturb you. But, *yes*, it has been one of those days. Why are you still here?"

"Just supporting my team," said Ellen quietly. "They're all out at a cocktail party with a client. And I'm staying late to finish their work. For me, this is a typical day."

"Oh, Ellen," said Marie, shaking her head. "I don't know how you've put up with it all these years.

"I need the paycheck," she said. "And so do you. It's just the way it is."

"Well," said Marie, "I'm looking forward to a big presentation this Friday. Zack promised that I could share my ideas. I've done a lot for it, so I'm pretty excited."

"I'm sure you have," said Ellen. "And good for you. For me, however, there is a line between the cubicle and the office," she whispered. "And I'm *never* going to cross it."

Chapter 13

A Terrible Injustice

For the following three days, Marie worked very long hours. She met with the team a few times. However, Zack didn't mention the presentation when Marie was there. Unlike the others, she had never seen it at the office. When she had a question or a comment about the presentation, Zack interrupted her in a patronizing* voice. "We'll get to that later, Marie," he said. "I need you to do something else right now." Then, with a false sense of urgency, Zack quickly sent her away to make unnecessary phone calls, write unimportant e-mails, and, of course, pick up his clean shirts from the laundry.

On Friday morning, Marie put on her new, perfectly tailored black suit and sea green blouse. Even though she bought her clothes at a discount store, they looked very nice. She put on a pair of tasteful earrings and took extra time with her hair and makeup. The result was quite respectable—and lovely. Marie looked like a person who was ready to take her rightful place *on* a PR team. Certainly, she had earned—or was about to earn—her way out of the cubicle. As Marie organized her briefcase, she carefully reviewed what she planned to say. After all, Zack had faithfully promised that she could speak directly to Eliza Adams' representatives at the appointed time.

The meeting in the executive boardroom began at exactly 11:00a.m. There were fifteen people around the long table: four representatives from Eliza Adams, Zack, the seven members of his team, senior partners Jacob Emerson and

Ruth Gables, and Marie. First, Zack told Marie to turn off the lights in the room. Then the presentation was projected onto a large screen against the wall. Zack proudly directed everyone's attention to Marie's presentation, without saying it was her work. Everything was the same. There were no changes in the content, the graphics, or the music. There was an impressive list of activities that contained information about press conferences, media announcements, promotions, advertising, and guest appearances by Eliza Adams. It briefly outlined the store's grand opening on 5th Avenue. And it had all of Marie's other ideas, including the drawing for the gown and the turquoise fireworks display.

Unfortunately, Zack never stopped speaking for a moment. With his eye on Marie's notes, he didn't let her or any other member of his team say a word. Marie tried a couple of times to get Zack's attention. "Now would be a good time," she thought, "to allow someone *else* to talk." But it never happened. And there was no way Marie could interrupt him without appearing unprofessional and foolish. At the end of the presentation, nearly an hour later, Zack received thunderous applause. "Bravo!" cried Niles, one of the client's representatives. "That was very well done!"

"Great job, Zack," said Jacob Emerson, getting up to shake Zack's hand. Following the presentation, there was some discussion at the table. The client's representatives had many questions. But Zack had his team members answer most of them. Zack asked Marie only one thing: "Would you turn the lights back on?" Marie felt disappointed and utterly used. Zack, however, was triumphant.

It was about 12:30p.m. when the Greek restaurant delivered the food for their lunch. "Oh," said Zack, in a soft voice that didn't actually get everyone's attention. "I hope you all have an appetite. And I must mention that Marie Durand has brought us this lunch—with the help of the great cooks at *Athena's* restaurant."

A few people looked up and smiled. Marie was horrified. Was this the acknowledgment she had been waiting for? Was Zack giving her credit for ordering the *food*? Marie couldn't believe this was happening. As the restaurant workers began to arrange some appetizing Greek dishes on a side table, Zack walked over to Marie. She couldn't look at him. He had lied to her. He had stolen her presentation. And even if it was good for business at *Emerson & Gables*, it just wasn't fair.

"Oh, Marie," said Zack, snapping his fingers at her. "It's your turn to talk now. Ask people what they want to drink—and bring it to them."

Chapter 14

Back to Vito's

Marie had three strong impulses. The first was to make a very loud announcement: "Zack had nothing to do with this presentation. These were all *my* ideas!" The second was to pour one of the messier Greek dishes directly onto Zack's head. And the third was to go to her cubicle, pick up the Canaletto print and African violet, and leave *Emerson & Gables* forever. It took every ounce of her self-control not to do any of these things. Instead, she obediently walked around the table and asked people for their drink orders. "What can I get for you?" she asked, just like she used to do at *Vito's*. For some reason, however, serving drinks in this room felt much, much worse. As she delivered beverages around the table, Evelyn asked, "Oh, can you please put a slice of lemon in my iced tea? You're the best, Marie."

Marie didn't stay for lunch. She had no appetite. She returned to her cubicle, sat down, and put her face in her hands. She was still in a state of shock. Then, silently, tears began to stream down her face. She opened her desk drawer to get a tissue. Inside, she found the note she had written on her first day: *1. Think happy thoughts. 2. Find a pretty picture of Venice.* Marie tore the paper into bits. She could no longer think positively. She had lost all hope. She had no future at *Emerson & Gables*. Her boss was a liar, and he wanted to trap her in this cubicle for the next thirty years.

All afternoon, Marie stayed at her desk. Somehow, she managed to get through some of the paperwork in front of her. She was sure Zack and his team were congratulating themselves. They were probably taking the rest of the day off. However, none of this really mattered anymore. If Marie was going to work here, she had to face the facts like Ellen had for all these years: "*It's just the way it is.*"

At exactly 5:00p.m., Marie got up from her chair. She didn't work one minute of overtime. She didn't chat with her co-workers in their cubicles. She didn't ask the team what they needed tomorrow. She just slipped out the glass doors and got onto the elevator. As the elevator went down to the lobby, Marie felt a pain in her stomach. Of course; she was hungry. She hadn't eaten a thing since early this morning.

Marie thought about the sad contents of the refrigerator in her apartment: wilted lettuce, and milk past its expiration date. Could she really go grocery shopping after a day like this? Outside, she saw the Number 8 Express bus going west. If she caught it, she could be at *Vito's* in just a few minutes. She desperately needed a plate of spaghetti with marinara sauce. And, more than that, she needed her surrogate mother and her old friends. Marie ran as fast as she could and got on the bus at the next stop.

Fifteen minutes later, Marie burst through the front door at *Vito's*.

"Well, look at you!" said a familiar figure. It was Tom Bertoli. "Power suit and everything," he said, smiling. "I *like* the corporate image. This is a big step up from the gray sweater on Sunday."

In spite of her dreadful mood, Marie laughed. As it had been a thoroughly depressing day, the laugh actually made her feel a lot better. "Thanks," she said. "Yeah, huge day in the PR business."

"PR?" said Tom. "I'm not sure what that means. Can you kindly explain it to me?"

"I'm afraid that you'll have to look it up in the dictionary," said Marie. "I'm too hungry to tell you about it right now. By the way, if you want to be a good *maître d'*, you'd better work on your people skills. You're rather sarcastic to the customers."

Tom laughed too. "Right this way, please," he said, leading her to a familiar table in the corner. "Oh, how many in your party?"

"One for now," said Marie. "But I'm hoping your mother can join me for a while. I've had a horrible day." Then Marie's emotions overtook her. The laughter disappeared. The smile was gone. And the tears reappeared. As Tom handed her the menu, Marie asked, "Is she free right now? I'd really like to talk to her."

Tom saw that these were not tears of laughter. He didn't try to make another joke. He looked very concerned. "I'm afraid she's not here this evening, Marie. She took the night off to take care of Lou's kids. I'm really sorry," said Tom. "Is there anything I can do to help?"

"Yes, please," said Marie, trying unsuccessfully to hide her emotions. "Can you give me back my old job?"

Chapter 15

Some Good Advice

"You don't mean that, do you?" asked Tom, as he brought Marie a glass of cold water. Then he sat down in the chair across from hers.

"I do, Tom. I really do," Marie said, holding the red napkin in front of her face. "I'm so sorry about this," she added tearfully. "This isn't your problem. Anyway, I know you're busy."

"I'm on a break," said Tom, without leaving his chair. "C'mon, Marie. You're part of the family, remember? What happened?"

Marie took a sip of her water and looked across the table at him. Once again, Marie noticed how incredibly handsome Tom was. His three-day beard was now shaved off, exposing his kind face and dark olive complexion*. All of the Bertolis were beautiful—inside and out. They *were* the salt of the earth. And what could be better than that? Marie was ashamed of the way she had judged them.

Just then Donna appeared at their table. She saw that Marie was upset and wrapped her arms around her. "Oh, honey," she said. "You look like you need some of *Vito's* medicine. Can I bring you all of your favorite foods?"

"Yes, please," sniffed Marie. "You're so nice." She wiped her eyes and tried to compose herself. "You see, Tom," said Marie, pointing toward Donna, who was now heading to the kitchen. "The workers here at *Vito's* are genuinely good people. They're not like that in the business world, where they lie, steal, and use you."

Although Tom tried hard to appear sympathetic, he smiled slightly at this melodramatic* account of life downtown. Marie smiled too. Then she laughed, in the strange way that someone can laugh and cry at the same time.

"I know bad things can happen at work sometimes," said Tom reassuringly. "But you have to accept that they do. Try not to let it upset you. You have to be tough."

"I don't want to be tough anymore," said Marie. "I expected life on the twenty-second floor of a fancy office building to be better. At first, I was impressed by it. But I'm not anymore. This is where I belong," she said, as Donna put a basket of warm bread and a green salad in front of her. "I want to come back to my dear friends and familiar surroundings. Every day, I want to look at the little mural of Venice in the banquet room. This is my home."

"Honey, your spaghetti with marinara sauce is on its way," Donna promised, before walking to another table. "Don't worry about a thing!"

"Thanks, Donna," said Marie. "You're wonderful."

Just then, Carlo came darting out from the kitchen. "I hear you're not feeling well, *signorina*," he said, kissing Marie on both cheeks. "Try the house red wine," he added, putting a glass in front of her.

"Thank you, Carlo," said Marie. "That's very sweet of you."

Marie stayed at *Vito's* until it closed at 10:00p.m. In that time frame, everyone—former co-workers and regular customers—came to welcome her. One delicious food after another appeared until Marie was too full to move—and too happy to care about Zack and everyone else at *Emerson & Gables*. When she attempted to pay, Tom said it was *on the house**.

"Okay," said Tom, giving her a hand up from the chair. "Donna, Carlo, and Joey are closing up tonight. Once again, I'm volunteering* to take you home."

"Thank you, Tom," said Marie, now in a much better mood. "I sincerely appreciate everything that you and everyone else did for me tonight. I feel so much happier now that I've made my decision."

"What decision?" asked Tom, as he opened the car door for her.

"I've decided to come back to work at *Vito's*!" said Marie cheerfully. "I should give my two weeks' notice at *Emerson & Gables*, of course. But can you get me on the schedule after that? You won't be sorry."

"But you'll be sorry," said Tom. "So we won't let you come back."

"What do you mean?" asked Marie, fastening her seatbelt. "Don't you want me here? Your mother knows that I'm a really good worker. Just ask her."

"I'm sure you are," said Tom gently. "My mother has already told me a lot about you, Marie. You worked very hard to make a change in your life—to move on from *Vito's*. You can't give up so soon."

"But Tom," said Marie, trying not to get emotional again. "I don't really want those things after all. I was looking for something that turned out to be nonsense. I'm much happier at *Vito's*. I really am."

"Marie, can I give you some *brotherly* advice?" Marie didn't answer, but she could feel the tears welling up in her eyes again. "You need to stand up for yourself in the business world, and everywhere else. Running away won't solve anything. Take it from me: *You have to get back on the horse that threw you.*"

Chapter 16

CD2

4

Two Very Different Messages

In the parked car, Tom and Marie talked for two more hours in front of her building. During that time, Marie learned a lot more about Tom Bertoli.

"As a kid, I started out in construction," he said. "Then I went to school, got a business degree, and worked in real estate development for several years in New York."

"Wow," said Marie. "That sounds interesting."

"Yes, Marie. Parts of that business are very interesting and rewarding. But there is a dark side to any job. I've also worked with some dishonest individuals, the ones who, as you said, *lie, steal, and use you.* Some people are good—and others are bad. What can I say? That's life. I know first–hand how stressful it can be."

"So, you got sick and tired of the stress," said Marie, looking intently into Tom's hazel eyes. "And you decided to come back to *Vito's.*"

"Well, yes and no," said Tom, smiling. "I was a little tired of living in New York. And I thought it was time to help my mother part-time at the restaurant. But I also moved back here for work. My partners and I are renovating* the old Channing Building on the waterfront. It's being turned into eco-friendly shops and condominiums*."

"Oh," said Marie, "I noticed a construction site there. Well, that's wonderful. Good for you."

"Thanks," said Tom. "But there are moments when I have regretted my involvement. It's a long and painful process. There can be very tense relationships with architects, engineers, contractors, construction workers, attorneys, government agents, bankers, and even PR people," he said with a wink. "There is *a lot* of money at stake. Everyone wants as much as he or she can get. And in the process, I have sometimes *lost* money. Believe me, there are times when I get frustrated and want to run away, too."

"But you don't," said Marie, "because you have to face your responsibilities. I get it."

"Yes, and the people in my development group have invested time and money, too. I can't think about turning back. Then, once a project is completed, I get a huge sense of satisfaction—even if I am sometimes poorer."

Marie smiled and looked at the moon through Tom's windshield. It was a beautiful, clear night. It seemed like a hundred years since Zack had humiliated her.

"You're right, Tom," said Marie. "And I have financial responsibilities, too. I can't just quit my job without having another one."

Tom looked directly into Marie's soulful brown eyes, thinking about how pretty she was.

"I should probably go in now," Marie said reluctantly, breaking Tom's gaze. "It's been a long day." She opened the car door. "I really appreciate your insight. I won't forget what you said."

"Don't mention it," said Tom. "It's been a pleasure talking to you. Maybe we can have dinner again—when the gray sweater is out of the laundry." Marie threw her head back and laughed very hard. Then they exchanged telephone numbers.

Marie got out of the car and walked upstairs to her small apartment. Inside, she took off her shoes and sat down on the sofa. She thought about everything Tom had said. He was really a great guy; humble*, hardworking, and sincere. He was the complete opposite of Zack, who was arrogant, lazy, and phony. Marie wondered how she could have ever admired him and his $200 hairstyle. Her earlier opinions were wrong; she had completely misjudged both men.

Before going to bed, Marie pulled her cell phone out of her purse and saw that she had two voicemail messages. The first message was from Mrs. Bertoli: "Hi, Marie. Donna told me that you were at the restaurant tonight. Sorry I wasn't there, but please know that you can always count on your *family* for support. We all love you. Never forget that. Call me later if you want to. Or come into *Vito's* again soon. I'll be there!"

The voice in the second message made her skin crawl. It was from Zack: "Hey, Marie. I didn't see you before you left today. The presentation went well, didn't it? Well, believe it or not, *Eliza Adams* is coming into the office *in person* next Friday! She wants more detailed plans for the grand opening of the store. And *you're* the person to think about that, right? So, I've sent you the latest version of the presentation. I know it's the weekend, but duty calls—especially when your goal is to be *on* my team…someday. Have some ideas to show me ASAP. Meanwhile, I'm at the *Hillsdale Resort & Spa. Ciao.* Oh, and one more thing: next time you're at the laundry, tell them I like medium starch on my shirts."

Chapter 17

Marie Plans Her Revenge

Early on Saturday morning, Marie opened her eyes and yawned. She stared at the cracks in the ceiling above her. She definitely lived in an old, run-down apartment. She had moved there about ten years ago with her father. After her father died, the landlord* agreed to keep the rent relatively low, but he certainly wasn't making any improvements. Marie wanted to move out of this shabby* place and away from its sad memories, but she didn't make a lot of money. An Assistant PR Coordinator's salary was not high. And she had to spend more money on clothes—even the ones at discount stores—than in the past. She barely earned more than her paycheck at *Vito's*.

Marie reached for her cell phone and listened to her messages again. She clearly remembered the very sweet words from Mrs. Bertoli, but perhaps she had only dreamed the ridiculous call from Zack. When she realized that it hadn't been a dream, she closed her eyes and sighed. So, after his shameful behavior, Zack now expected Marie to work all weekend. Then, of course, he would take all of the credit for her ideas. Apparently, that's the way things worked at *Emerson & Gables*. Ellen was right about their positions in the company: the managers liked them where they were—in cubicles—and their jobs were to make other people look good.

Zack's message didn't cause Marie to get angry. She didn't stamp her feet. She didn't throw her water glass against the wall. Zack's outrageous* request actually amused her—and then made her feel stronger. A smile slowly spread across her face. Right away, Marie began to form some plans of her own. "Yes, *I have to get back on the horse that threw me*," she thought cheerfully. "And he will *never* throw me again," she said aloud, leaping out of bed.

Right away, Marie set her laptop on the dining room table. She had to get busy. Eliza Adams expected detailed plans for the grand opening very soon. This project might take more than the whole weekend. Still, Marie knew what she had to do. As she crossed the living room to find her briefcase, the telephone rang. Not surprisingly, it was Zack.

"Hey, babe," he said casually. "Just wanted to make sure that you got my message."

"Oh, yes," said Marie. "I got it. I'm already working on it."

"Good girl!" said Zack enthusiastically. His language made Marie cringe*. "We have to amaze Eliza Adams when she comes. I can't believe that she'll be here in less than a week. Things are moving forward quickly... Ouch!" Zack shouted into the telephone. "Not so hard!" he said, to a person who wasn't Marie.

"Hello?" said Marie. "Are you there?" "Yes," said Zack, with annoyance. "I'm here. I'm getting a deep tissue massage, and it's *painful*. Anyway, when do you think you'll be finished?"

"I don't know," said Marie honestly. "It depends on the rest of my work schedule this week. If I'm dropping off your laundry, it may take a very long time. You know, Zack, maybe it would be better for *you* to handle the details of the grand opening." For a moment, Marie put her hand over her mouth to keep from laughing. "After all, you'll be presenting the ideas to Eliza Adams, right?"

"Well, *yes,*" said Zack. "I mean *no.* That won't work. I have too many things to do…Ouch!" he said again, "Sheesh, this massage really hurts! Okay, look. I promise that I'll give you more time in the office this week. And, of course, you'll get to share some of your thoughts with Eliza Adams." But Marie knew what Zack was really thinking. Even on the massage table, he was scheming. He would find a way to keep her away from the client on Friday. He would steal from her again. Zack wanted to keep Marie in the cubicle and *never* let her out.

"Well," said Marie, "if I'm not distracted by too many errands, I should be able to have everything ready by Friday."

"Good," said Zack. "But it needs to be *before* Friday. You know, to be on the safe side. You could get sick or something. Let's not wait until the last minute. So, promise me that you'll spend today, tomorrow, and next week preparing for it."

"Don't worry," said Marie calmly. "I want our client to be happy."

"Great," said Zack. "But I've got to go now. It's almost time for my facial."

Chapter 18

CD2

6

A Wonderful Evening

Marie began a schedule for the grand opening of the Eliza Adams store. She worked non-stop for almost six hours. As she was writing down the details for the ribbon-cutting ceremony, the telephone rang. It was Tom Bertoli. "I know this is a little last-minute," he said, "but would you like a tour of the Channing Building this evening? The construction crews aren't there on the weekend. Anyway, I thought you might find it interesting."

"I'd love to see it!" Marie exclaimed. "It will be a nice break from the huge project I'm working on."

"So, I'm guessing that you still have your job," said Tom.

"I do, indeed," said Marie, "But I wanted to quit again when I heard Zack's message last night. Believe it or not, he gave me an order from the *Hillsdale Resort & Spa*. I'm not exactly sure where he was at the time. He was either on the tennis court, in the pool, or on the golf course. Then he called again this morning from the massage table. Anyway, I must work this weekend and beyond, I'm afraid."

"Ah, the evil boss strikes again!" said Tom. "Will you be too busy to have dinner with me afterward? It's not a fancy place. In fact, old gray sweaters are pretty much the required dress code."

Marie laughed and felt her heart flutter. "I would really enjoy that, Tom," she said. "And I need the break. I'm tired of being cooped up in this apartment. It's beginning to feel like my cubicle," she added. "Thank you for the excuse to get out." After they agreed on a time to meet, Marie hung up the phone. For a moment, she looked guiltily at her computer. Then she defiantly shut it down and closed the top. "Zack certainly made time for himself today," thought Marie, "and so will I."

At 6:00p.m., Marie met Tom outside her building. He was standing on the sidewalk waiting for her. "I ironed my shirt," he said, smiling. "I hope you approve." Once again, Marie laughed. Tom was so funny. And how refreshing* it was to spend time with a genuinely nice man—in addition to a very handsome one. She felt ashamed of what she had thought before. Tom was better than Zack in every respect.

As they drove toward the Channing Building, Tom saw that Marie wasn't wearing her old gray sweater; she was dressed in a light blue blouse and black skirt. She had a silver sweater draped over her arm. They made easy conversation all the way down to the waterfront. Tom parked the car across from the Channing Building and led her to the entrance.

"This place was built in 1893," said Tom, fumbling for a key. "That's ancient history here in the U.S.," he added with a smile. "It had been abandoned for many years and was in very bad shape. Our development group was overjoyed to get the contract. I love seeing a place like this come back to life."

Marie looked up admiringly at the old brick structure. Since they stood on some wobbly plywood instead of a finished walkway, Tom reached for Marie's hand to guide her through the entrance. He didn't let go of it right away once they were inside. His warm hand felt so good around hers—like it had belonged there always. Their hands remained together until Tom found the light switch. Then Marie reluctantly let go.

"There will be three businesses down here," Tom explained, gesturing toward the large open space. "We have signed leases for an organic grocery store, a "green*" coffee shop, and a natural-fibers clothing store. All of the businesses are "eco-friendly*," just like the twenty-four condos* above us. Things are moving quickly now. In about nine months, these businesses will be running, and there will be many tenants upstairs. Would you like to see a living space? There's one on the fourth floor. We're using it as a model when it's finished."

"Yes!" said Marie, excitedly. She and Tom took the elevator to the fourth floor. They walked down the hall to an end unit, and Tom unlocked the door to a nearly completed condo. It had an incredible view of the bay.

"This is it," said Tom proudly. "Everything is made from sustainable* wood products and non-toxic materials. You know, no harm to the environment and that sort of thing." He showed her the different areas: living room, dining room, kitchen, two bedrooms and two bathrooms. Marie was very impressed.

"It's just beautiful," she said, looking around and then pausing to gaze out the window. "And what a gorgeous view!" On the bay, she focused on a little red sailboat among the other boats in the water. "I can see why your work is so rewarding."

"It generally is," said Tom. "And in a few months, we'll need a good PR agency for advertising. What about *Emerson & Gables*? I've heard there are a few competent people working there. Should I contact Zack when he has a moment on the massage table?" Tom smiled.

"Or you can contact *Marie*," she replied, her eyes shining. "You'll probably find her in the cubicle, but she'll gladly do everything she can to help you."

Chapter 19

A Personal Day for Marie

On Monday morning, Zack appeared at Marie's cubicle before 8:00a.m. "What do you have to show me?" he asked eagerly.

"I'm not finished," said Marie. "I worked all weekend on the grand opening, but I still have a lot to do. By the way, Zack, you're looking very tanned and relaxed."

"Thanks," said Zack, pulling a little hand mirror out of his pocket and looking into it. "I'm a little red from the facial. But the skin exfoliation* process is kind of rough. You should try it sometime, Marie. It can make you look years younger."

Marie felt her blood pressure go up. "Sadly, I don't have the time and money to spend at a spa," she replied curtly. "Lately, I've spent most of my free time working. Sorry if it has aged me." But Zack had stopped listening. When a subject was not about him, Zack had no interest in it. Marie abruptly turned back to her computer. She had made it clear that, for now, she wasn't ready to show her plans. As other workers had started to enter their cubicles, Zack skulked back to his office.

For the next two days, Zack didn't bother Marie. The team left her alone, too. No one dropped piles of work on her desk. Mateo had to return his own phone calls. Silvia had to do her own research. And Evelyn had to find her own lemon slices for her iced tea. Marie was busy doing other things to support them—and that was that. By Wednesday, however, Zack had become very anxious.

"I need to see something, Marie," he said, reappearing in her cubicle just before she left work. "Eliza Adams will be here on Friday afternoon, and I need to practice what you've prepared. Can you give me the plans now?"

"I suppose," said Marie, "but I'm still working on some *very* important details. You want this to be really good, don't you Zack? I can promise you that the end result will be worth it. You'll see it soon."

"Okay," said Zack with a sigh. "I have other things to do this evening anyway. Oh, um, can you run to the dry cleaners and pick up my blue suit?" he asked, pulling a white ticket from his wallet.

"Sure," Marie replied. "But that means I'll have a little less time to work on the presentation at home. Your call, Zack."

"Never mind," he said, putting away his ticket. "Go home and do what you have to do. But send me the presentation the moment you finish it." He flashed his blinding smile and reached over to touch Marie's hair, but she backed away from him.

"Yes," said Marie, "I'll do what I have to do."

Marie went directly home. She turned on the computer to review her work. Every moment of the grand opening had been carefully planned: the mayor's address to the crowd, Eliza's arrival in a turquoise convertible, the spectacular fashion show on an outdoor stage, the ribbon-cutting ceremony, the drawing for the new gown, and every last firework. Marie had estimated costs for everything. Her ideas were original and well thought out. The grand opening was going to be the most exciting event in the history of 5th Avenue. Marie had no doubt that Eliza Adams would be pleased.

The next morning Marie did something that she had never, ever done at *Emerson & Gables*: she took a day off. She knew Zack would be frantic*, but she didn't care. She was entitled to some personal days each year, and she wanted to use one. In the morning, she left the following message on Zack's machine: "Hello, Zack. It's Marie. I'm completely exhausted, so I'm not coming in today. Everyone needs to *de-stress* now and then. Don't worry. I'll have the grand opening plans tomorrow."

When Zack heard Marie's message, he flew into a rage. His face turned redder than it had after his facial. He shouted a string of very bad words, then he threw his phone across the room.

When Zack heard Marie's message, he flew into a rage.

Evelyn heard the commotion and ran toward his office. "My gosh, Zack! What's wrong?" she asked in alarm.

"Everything," said Zack, growing even angrier. "Marie took a personal day today."

"Oh," said Evelyn, not understanding why this was so terrible. "Well, that's not the end of the world, is it?"

"Yes, it is!" said Zack, slamming his fist on the desk. "She has the grand opening plans—and I don't."

"Why does *she* have them?" asked Evelyn.

"Because *she* wrote them," said Zack. "Never mind, Evelyn," he barked. "This is really none of your business. Get out of here and leave me alone!"

Chapter 20

Zack's Temper Tantrum

Zack's temper tantrum escalated*. He angrily swept papers from his desk onto the floor. He overturned his office chair. He kicked a hole in the wall. And he uprooted a lovely indoor ficus tree, shaking dirt and leaves everywhere. His co-workers on the twenty-second floor heard his shouting and swearing. His behavior frightened Evelyn and everyone near him. She quickly called security and then alerted both Jacob Emerson and Ruth Gables. "Zack is out of control!" she said urgently. "Please hurry!"

The senior partners, both in their mid-sixties, ran out of their offices and toward Zack's. At the sight of them—and the sudden realization that he had attracted a crowd—Zack began to calm down.

"Zack!" said Ruth sternly, looking at the destruction in his office. "What on earth is going on in here?"

"Ugh," said Zack awkwardly, trying to catch his breath. He still had the ficus tree in his hands. "It's just one of those days, you know?"

"No, we absolutely don't know," said Jacob. "In any case, your reaction to a bad day is not acceptable."

"Is everything okay in here?" asked the security officer who had suddenly appeared on the scene.

"Yes," said Zack, now very embarrassed. "Everything is fine," he insisted, quickly putting down the tree and attempting to smooth down his $200 hairstyle. "The show is over!" he snapped at the dozen people outside his doorway. "Go back to work!" He looked down at the floor, now

65

covered in paper, dirt, and ficus tree leaves. Nevertheless, the security officer remained where he was.

"Can you please explain this?" asked Ruth.

"I got some bad news," said Zack, his face still a bright red. "That's all. I guess I overreacted*."

"That is not a satisfactory explanation," said Ruth, crossing her arms with annoyance.

"You know that Eliza Adams is flying in from London tonight," Zack said.

"Of course we know that," said Jacob. "We'll be at your team's presentation for her tomorrow. You've planned the grand opening events, haven't you?"

Zack shifted his feet back and forth on the carpet, almost like he was doing a little dance. "Well," he replied, "it's true that our team has done some research. But our assistant, Marie Durand, has prepared the *details* of the event. And, uh, Marie isn't here today because she took a personal day. And I'm upset because she isn't here."

Jacob and Ruth looked confused. "I know Marie," said Ruth. "She's a very good worker. But she didn't prepare the whole presentation, did she? She's an Assistant PR Coordinator, Zack. That's far too much responsibility for someone with so little experience. What were you thinking?"

"I thought that she would do a good job—and be here like she promised," Zack said, kicking a paper on the floor in anger. The security guard stepped forward, but Zack just waved him away. Jacob shook his head in disgust.

"That was badly managed, Zack. We have a major client coming here tomorrow. And now you're telling me that Marie, from the cubicle, may or may not have something to show her?"

"Now you know *why* I'm mad," said Zack, smugly flashing a bitter white smile. "She let me down. I was supposed to be practicing today."

"You shouldn't have been practicing *her* presentation, Zack," said Ruth. "You and your team were responsible for creating that work. We could lose the Eliza Adams account over this."

"Well, you see, Marie had done an excellent job on the first presentation. So I trusted her to do these plans too," Zack said.

Jacob took off his glasses and looked at Zack in disbelief. "Are you telling me that she did the presentation for the client's representatives last week?" he asked.

"Yes," said Zack defensively. "I told you she was good. Surprisingly good, really."

"So *you* presented *her* work," said Jacob, "and *she* took our drink orders? I've never heard of anything so ridiculous."

"In the meantime," said Ruth, "we can't expect Eliza Adams' plane to turn around. And although this is bad news, it wasn't helpful to disturb an entire office and hurt an innocent ficus tree. For now, Zack, you need to clean up this mess," she said, pointing a finger at him. "And we'll assess the damages later," she added, looking at the hole in the wall. As Ruth and Jacob left the room, Jacob turned to the security guard. "Please stay here until he's finished."

Chapter 21

Marie Makes an Impression

On Friday morning, Marie woke up very early. She felt refreshed after using her personal day to *de-stress*. She didn't have a massage, and she didn't have a facial, but she did take a long walk along the waterfront. She noticed several construction workers around the Channing Building. Naturally, she thought of Tom. She recalled the moment when his hand reached for hers last Saturday. The memory gave her the same warm sensation. Even so, she wasn't entirely sure about Tom's feelings for her. They clearly enjoyed each other's company, but perhaps the attraction wasn't mutual. It was possible that Tom saw her as nothing more than a younger sister. Regardless*, she couldn't worry about that right now. She had a big day ahead at work.

Marie arrived at *Emerson & Gables* thirty minutes early. Once again, she was wearing her black suit, this time accessorized with a pretty pink blouse. At her cubicle, she found a handwritten note from Ruth Gables taped to her phone. It read: "Please report to me immediately." The message worried Marie. Was she in trouble for taking a personal day? Was she getting fired for not delivering the presentation? With her stomach churning, Marie picked up her laptop and went directly to Ruth's office. Both Ruth and Jacob Emerson were waiting for her.

"Good morning, Marie," said Ruth kindly. "Please sit down." Marie nervously did as she was told. "You weren't here yesterday," Ruth added. "So you missed an ugly scene with your manager, Zack. He was very upset because you hadn't sent him the grand opening plans. You remember that our client is coming this afternoon."

"I realize that," said Marie honestly. "But I have the completed plans here on my laptop. Would you like to see them?"

"We certainly would," said Jacob. "Please share them with us."

For the next hour, Marie eloquently shared her plans for the grand opening. The high quality of her work proved that she was the same person who had created the presentation for the client's representatives last week. Both Jacob and Ruth were very impressed.

"So, you've done *this* in your cubicle," said Ruth.

"Well, partly," replied Marie. "I've done a lot of it at home. Zack and his team give me other things to do here." The senior partners both shook their heads. "I realize that I'm new at this job," said Marie. "However, my goal is to be *on* a PR team someday. I just wanted you to know that I am capable of doing good work. But I understand if you would like Zack to present my ideas to the client," said Marie.

"Why would we want Zack to present *your* work?" said Ruth. "I think you've earned the right to do that yourself."

◆ ◆ ◆

At two-o'clock on Friday, Eliza Adams walked through the glass doors with the gold lettering: *Emerson & Gables, Public Relations*. She was about fifty years old and had jet-black hair pulled tightly into a bun. She wore an emerald green suit from her collection, accessorized with expensive jewelry. Eliza was led immediately to the conference room. This time, there were sixteen people around the long table: Eliza Adams, her four representatives, Zack, the seven members of his team, Jacob, Ruth, and Marie. First, Ruth told Zack to serve drinks to everyone around the table. She also told him to turn off the lights in the room. Next, Jacob proudly introduced Marie and directed everyone's attention to *her* work. Then, the grand opening plans were projected onto a large screen against the wall. Finally, Marie confidently presented *her* ideas as only she could.

Marie confidently presented her ideas as only she could.

At the end of the presentation, everyone applauded wildly. Zack clapped slowly. The members of his team looked at each other uncomfortably. Eliza Adams jumped out of her chair and embraced Marie. "That was brilliant, darling!" she said effusively*. "We must have Marie in charge of everything for the grand opening. What delightful ideas you have! I love the fashion show on the outdoor stage. And the turquoise fireworks! It must be our blueprint* for other cities too."

"Thank you very much," said Marie. "I've really enjoyed working on your account."

"When this general meeting is over," said Eliza, "my staff and I would like to talk to you in your office. There are some things that I'd like to discuss in a smaller group."

Marie looked at Jacob and Ruth uncertainly.

"Oh, please use my office," said Ruth. "Marie's office is… well…a little small."

Chapter 22

Ellen Crosses the Line

Three months later, Marie had no more doubts about Tom's feelings. He didn't really see her as a younger sister; he was, in fact, madly in love with her. And the feeling was mutual.

This relationship delighted Mrs. Bertoli for a number of reasons: she saw her dear Marie more frequently at *Vito's* and in her own home. Tommaso was much happier now that he was no longer *desperately lonely*. And it allowed her the satisfaction of clapping her hands together and exclaiming, "I always *knew* the two of you would hit it off!" Although they were both very busy, Marie and Tom saw or spoke to each other every single day. She wanted to know everything that happened inside the Channing Building and at *Vito's* restaurant, and he enjoyed the daily soap opera at *Emerson & Gables*.

As with any good drama, the villain* was punished. Zack was fired two weeks after the meeting with Eliza Adams. His temper tantrum was one reason. And, of course, he had poorly managed his time, his team, and Marie. But his worst offense was misusing the company credit card. His bills for restaurants, golf games, and resorts were not, in fact, *business expenses**: they were seen as *theft*, so his employment was terminated. Zack had to repay his large debts. He was also billed for the cleaning and repair of his office—and a new ficus tree. Then two security officers escorted him from the building.

Marie's career moved in the opposite direction. Soon after the successful meeting with Eliza Adams, great things began to happen. Marie was offered a pay rise and an outer office with a view. It wasn't Zack's corner office, but it was a huge improvement. It took only a few minutes to move. She hurriedly packed up her desk, file drawers, Canaletto print, and African violet. Jacob and Ruth also asked her to form her own PR team.

"May I please recruit Ellen Jenkins?" Marie asked. "She's a very hard worker and a great employee. I'll gladly share my new office with her."

When she heard the happy news, a tearful Ellen hugged Marie with gratitude.

"Thank you, Marie!" said Ellen. "I've finally crossed the line! I can't tell you how much I appreciate this opportunity— and the chance to work with you."

Later, Marie heroically supported Eliza Adams at all of the events connected to the grand opening of her new store. Eliza insisted that Marie accompany her to every television appearance, radio interview, and other promotional outing. Eliza trusted Marie to be on top of everything—and she was. Unlike Eliza, Marie was always calm. She knew exactly where Eliza had to be and what she had to say and do. Everything went well, and news of the grand opening spread quickly throughout the city.

The grand opening event was an enormous success. Thousands of excited people crowded together along 5th Avenue. Everything went according to plan, from Eliza's unforgettable arrival in the turquoise convertible to the very last turquoise firework. "This is, by far, the very best grand opening we've ever had. And that's a great credit to you, Marie," Eliza said sincerely. "I know you worked very hard to plan and publicize this event. I am so grateful to you."

"The pleasure was all mine," said Marie. "And I know that your store will do well in our city."

As the evening came to an end, Tom finally found Marie in the crowd. He wrapped his strong arms around her and gave her a congratulatory* kiss. Eliza Adams was nearby with her staff, so Marie pulled Tom in her direction. "Eliza, I'd like you to meet my boyfriend, Tom Bertoli. And Tom, this is my client—and now very good friend—Eliza Adams."

They shook hands warmly. "It's very nice to meet you," said Tom happily. "This evening was fantastic. Best wishes for your success here."

"It's lovely to meet you, too," said Eliza. "And thank you. Marie is such a wonderful, talented young woman. This whole night was her idea. You're a lucky man, Tom—but I'll bet you already know that." Eliza then turned to Marie and whispered in her ear. "He's just adorable. You two make a *beautiful* couple. And when the time comes for a wedding dress, you're going to wear one of my designs. And don't even think about the price tag—it's on me!"

Chapter 23

An Amazing Surprise

One year later, Marie and Tom were walking hand in hand along the waterfront. It was two weeks before their wedding. They were a very happy couple, and enjoyed each other's company in every way. They had more than just a physical attraction; Marie had never laughed so much in her whole life before she met Tom, and Tom thought that Marie was the smartest woman in the world. He told her that he was in love from the moment she defined PR. Although their first meeting was a longstanding joke, Tom truly admired Marie for her strength and intelligence.

"Sorry, but I don't think it was love at first sight for me," said Marie. "I felt a little hurt by your response: *'I have heard of public relations. And I know what people in PR do.'* But it was definitely love at second sight. I really fell for you that night at *Vito's*—even though you refused to give me back my old job."

Tom laughed. "It's pretty windy out here now," he said. "Let's go inside the Channing Building and look around."

Marie and Tom crossed the street and saw the busy shops that were now open on the first floor. They walked inside the coffee shop and ordered two coffees and some pastries. Naturally, the topic of their upcoming wedding came up. Tom said, "For a person who worries about big events for her clients, you don't seem very worried about our wedding."

"I'm not," said Marie.

"You've never been upset about the food, flowers, or the shade of red my mother is wearing. Why aren't you acting like a *bridezilla**?"

"Because I'm marrying you, Tom," said Marie with a big smile. "That's all I care about. In this case, I don't care about the details. I don't need perfection. I don't need fireworks. I'm just thrilled to spend the rest of my life with you."

This time, it was Tom who had tears in his eyes.

"Before we walk back to the car, I'd like to show you one more thing upstairs," he said.

"Are you sure?" asked Marie. "It's getting kind of late. Aren't you supposed to help at *Vito's* tonight?"

"Not tonight," said Tom. "Mom knows we're busy. She's giving me the night off." Marie and Tom entered the building through another doorway. The walkway was no longer wobbly plywood, but Tom still held Marie's hand tightly. "All of the condos are sold," Tom said proudly. "But you must see the last one."

They took the elevator to the fourth floor. From his pocket, Tom pulled out a key for the same unit Marie had seen many months before. "This is it!" he said.

"I remember this place," said Marie, stepping inside. "How stunning it is now that it's finished! Lucky people," she said enviously as she looked at the beautiful kitchen cabinets, the new appliances, the decorative light fixtures, and the gorgeous bamboo floors. Then she walked over toward the window. "Gosh, look at the amazing view of the bay."

"Yes, pretty nice," said Tom.

"You should be really proud of this place, darling. The whole building is a work of art. But should we be in here, Tom?" asked Marie, noting a pretty red sofa in the living room. "It looks like the people have begun to move in."

"Yes, it's fine. Believe me. You have to see their finished walk-in closet."

"Are you sure?" Marie asked nervously.

"Definitely," said Tom. "Just one more thing."

Marie walked into the master bedroom, which had an equally breathtaking view of the bay. She turned the knob on the closet door. It was indeed very large. It was probably ten times the size of the one in her little apartment. The closet was empty except for one thing: her old gray sweater. Marie turned around and stared at Tom in disbelief.

"I've grown rather fond of that old sweater," he said. "I hope you wear it often. Of course, we'll also have plenty of room in here for your power suit—and your wedding gown."

Marie was still unable to speak. "My mother told me that you liked surprises," Tom added. "I really hope you like this one. And don't worry. I actually made some money on this project. We can afford it."

Marie put one hand over her mouth and the other over her heart. Then, her eyes overflowing with tears, she fell into Tom's arms.

Chapter 24

In Venice

Two weeks later, there were many more tears of joy. There was not a dry eye among the guests at Marie and Tom's wedding ceremony. Everyone came: the entire staff at *Vito's*, Marie's good friends from *Emerson & Gables*, including Ellen, Ruth, and Jacob. The entire Bertoli family was there along with many of their lifelong friends. Eliza Adams flew in all the way from England. She wanted to do the final fitting of Marie's dress herself. "I insist, dear Marie," she said, in a phone call from London. "I know what I'm doing. And you will be the most beautiful bride that ever was."

On the wedding day, Mrs. Bertoli played two roles: mother of the bride and mother of the groom. "Marie," she said before the ceremony, "I know that your real parents would be so proud of you. Thank you for the privilege of walking you down the aisle in their place. Our family is so happy to *officially* welcome you. I know that my husband, Vito, is…" Mrs. Bertoli couldn't finish her sentence. She had to stop and compose herself. "… smiling down on us." Marie embraced her surrogate mother and—almost—mother-in-law.

"Thank you," said Marie, trying hard not to cry. "I wouldn't have made it without your love and support all these years. I am the luckiest person in the world." Marie took a moment to reflect on her unbelievable journey. "Eight years ago," she thought, "I was a desperate nineteen-year-old girl who wandered into a restaurant…and now here I am." Today she was marrying Tom, Mrs. Bertoli's son, the best man in the whole world.

The wedding reception was at *Vito's*, of course. The restaurant was closed to the public for the event. The wedding guests occupied the entire dining room as well as the new outdoor patio area. Marie and Tom posed for several pictures in front of her favorite mural in the banquet room. There was an array of her favorite Italian food and a seven-layer red velvet cake. Red orchids were everywhere. A band, featuring an amazing accordion player, played festive Italian music. Their guests danced. She had never seen a group of people have more fun, especially Carlo and Eliza Adams, who danced the Tarantella together. Marie and Tom were overwhelmed with happiness.

◆ ◆ ◆

A week later, Marie and Tom sat at an outdoor café in Italy. "My life is an unbelievably good dream," said Marie, watching boats go by on the Grand Canal. "I've wanted to see Venice all my life."

"Where else would we go on our honeymoon*?" asked Tom, as he swept up some seafood linguine with his fork and spoon. "You know, I've eaten a lot of Italian food in my life, but this is really incredible. You have to taste this," he said, passing a bite to Marie. "It's much better than my mother's seafood linguine. Don't tell her, though. I don't want a plate of it poured onto my head."

"I'll *never* tell her," said Marie. "It is delicious," she added. "And you must try my farfalle with mushrooms and shallots. We need something like this on the menu at *Vito's*. It actually seems very healthy."

"*My life is an unbelievably good dream. I've wanted to see Venice all my life.*"

Marie and Tom finished their dinner, paid the bill, and walked hand in hand toward the Rialto Bridge. It was evening now and the lights of the city looked magical. Tom pointed to a boat dock a few yards ahead.

"That's where we catch our gondola," he said. "I know it's kind of touristy*—and a bit expensive—but it's our honeymoon, right?"

"Yes, we must do it," said Marie. "It's all part of the experience."

"Get ready," said Tom, leading her down to the boat. "I'm going to ask the poor gondolier to sing *O Sole Mio*. And I mean every word of it, honey," he said, leaning over to kiss Marie. "I don't know all of the words. But there is something about the sad feeling one has when the sun goes down. Then there is another sun that's brighter...and it's the one on your face."

"Oh, Tom. You are so romantic," Marie said, her eyes glistening with tears. "I love you with all my heart."

Just then the gondolier helped them climb aboard. The full moon shone down brightly on the Grand Canal. "And just look at our boat, Tom!" Marie observed emotionally. Once again, she laughed, the strange way that someone can laugh and cry at the same time. "It's red!"

E X E R C I S E S

A Comprehension

Chapters 1 – 6 Are these sentences true (T) or false (F)?

1 Marie didn't like working at Vito's. **T / F**

2 Ellen and Marie didn't have the same job title. **T / F**

3 Zack asked Marie to do things that weren't in her job description. **T / F**

4 Marie's father left her enough money for her college tuition when he died. **T / F**

5 Marie wasn't interested in meeting Mrs. Bertoli's son, Tom. **T / F**

6 Marie had a lot of ideas for the Eliza Adams account. **T / F**

Chapters 7 – 12 Who said each of these sentences and to whom?

7 "Don't worry about it. I'll order for both of us."

8 "I'd really like to help with the presentation next week."

9 "I finished the salad when you were in the shower. And the garlic bread is nearly ready."

10 "I wasn't expecting any company tonight. Sorry for being a bit antisocial."

11 "You do such a great job supporting us, Marie. We would be lost without you."

12 "For me, however, there is a line between the cubicle and the office. And I'm *never* going to cross it."

Chapters 13 – 18 Put these events in the correct order.

13 Tom tells Marie that she needs to stand up for herself and refuses to give her back her job.

14 Zack leaves Marie a message and tells her to make a more detailed presentation.

15 Tom takes Marie to see his construction project and tells her about his plans.

16 Zack calls Marie from the spa and she decides how she will get her revenge on him.

17 Zack doesn't let Marie talk in the meeting and makes her serve drinks instead.

18 Marie goes to *Vito's* and asks Tom to give her back her job.

Chapters 19 – 24 In this part of the story, when and why does:

19 Marie feel confident?

20 Zack feel furious?

21 Ruth feel impressed?

22 Ellen feel grateful?

23 Tom feel overwhelmed?

24 Marie feel tearful?

B Working with Language

I Match the adjectives in column A with the corresponding words or phrases in column B.

A	B
breathtaking	Marie's high school French
sustainable and eco-friendly	Mrs. Bertoli's sons
shabby and loose-fitting	Ellen's training style
rusty	The view of the bay
creative and competent	Marie's old gray sweater
honest, decent and unpretentious	The wood products in Tom's condos

2 Complete the paragraph by filling the gaps with the options in the box below. Two options are not needed.

> refused to spend   unlike Ellen   advance her career
> determined to   to be promoted   deserved
> planned to impress   as smart and capable as

Marie rightly believed that she was _____
everyone on Zack's team – including Zack. Therefore, she
_____ an eternity in the cubicle. _____,
she was not going to wait patiently _____
someday. Marie was _____ climb the corporate
ladder. She _____ more money and a better view.

C Activities

1 "Since beginning her new job, Marie had become interested in a different type of man. He wasn't an auto mechanic, a plumber or a construction worker. Instead, he wore an expensive suit and had a $200 hairstyle." (page 18)
Do you think Marie's prejudice against working-class men was reasonable? Why / Why not?

2 Imagine you are Marie or Tom. Write a postcard or an email to Mrs. Bertoli from Venice.

GLOSSARY

amateurish *(adj)* done in an unprofessional or unskilled way

appalling *(adj)* horrifying or shocking

blueprint *(n)* something which acts as a plan or template for other things

boorish *(adj)* very bad-mannered

bridezilla *(n)* a woman who behaves in an obsessive and demanding way while planning her wedding

buddies *(n)* slang term for 'friends', particularly in American English

business expenses *(n)* costs to an employee, e.g. taking a client out for dinner, which are reimbursed by the company

busser *(n)* American English slang term for the person who clears tables in a restaurant

clerical *(adj)* relating to work in an office, especially administration

compile *(vb)* to put together e.g. a list of information

complexion *(n)* the natural appearance of a person's skin

condescending *(adj)* showing an attitude of superiority

condominium (condo) *(n)* a building containing lots of individually owned apartments, or condos

congratulatory *(adj)* in a way that demonstrates congratulations

corporate ladder *(n)* to 'climb the corporate ladder' is to be promoted up through a company from an entry-level position to an executive position

cringe *(vb)* to experience an inward shiver of embarrassment or disgust

eco-friendly *(adj)* good for the environment

effusively *(avb)* in a way that shows a lot of emotion

entry-level position *(n)* the lowest position in a company, not requiring any experience

escalate *(vb)* to rapidly increase or become more serious

feign *(vb)* to pretend

frantic *(adj)* extremely frightened or anxious

green *(adj)* good for the environment

haughtily *(avb)* with arrogance, superiority

honeymoon *(n)* the holiday a newly married couple take after their wedding

humble *(adj)* showing that you think you are less important than others

hybrid *(n)* a mix of two or more different elements; a hybrid car is part electric, so more eco-friendly

insecure *(adj)* unsure or anxious about yourself

IT *(n)* abbreviation for 'Information Technology'; relating to computers

landlord *(n)* a person who rents accommodation to others

melodramatic *(adj)* exaggerated, over-emotional

meticulous *(adj)* very careful and precise, with great attention to detail

on the house *(adj)* given to someone for free by a business

outrageous *(adj)* shockingly bad

overreact *(vb)* to react too strongly to something

overwhelming *(adj)* enormous, difficult to cope with

patronizing *(adj)* in a way that shows a feeling of superiority

peek *(vb)* to look at something quickly or secretly

probationary period *(n)* a period of assessment or supervision in a new job

phony *(adj)* fake; false

potential *(n)* showing the capacity to develop

promote *(vb)* to raise someone to a higher position within a company

refreshing *(adj)* when something is welcome or stimulating because it is new or different

regardless *(avb)* without consideration for

renovate *(vb)* to restore something to a better state

rusty *(adj)* of a low standard because of a lack of recent practice

sarcastically *(avb)* saying the opposite of what you mean in order to mock someone

shabby *(adj)* in a poor condition due to lack of care

surrogate *(adj)* someone that takes the place of someone else

sustainable *(adj)* able to continue for a long time

touristy *(adj)* particularly well-visited by tourists

underling *(n)* a person of lower status

unpretentious *(adj)* not attempting to impress others by trying to appear more important

verge *(n)* the very edge

villain *(n)* the person in a story responsible for harm or trouble

volunteer *(vb)* to offer to do something, in return for nothing

wistfully *(avb)* with a feeling of sad regret

A N S W E R   K E Y

A Comprehension

Chapters 1 – 6

1 F   **2** F   **3** T   **4** F   **5** T   **6** T

Chapters 7 – 12

7 Zack to Marie   **8** Marie to Zack   **9** Mrs. Bertoli to Tom

10 Tom to Marie   **11** Evelyn to Marie   **12** Ellen to Marie

Chapters 13 – 18

5, 6, 1, 2, 4, 3

Chapters 19 – 24

19 When she has prepared her excellent presentation and has a plan, because she knows that she has done well.

20 When he finds out that Marie has taken the day off work, because he has no work of his own prepared.

21 When she hears Marie's presentation, because Marie has done an excellent job.

22 When Marie invites her to be on her PR team, because she is so happy to get out of her cubicle.

23 When he takes Marie to see the new apartment, because Marie says such loving things to him.

24 When she and Tom are on their honeymoon, because she is so happy.

B Working with Language

1

breathtaking – The view from the bay

sustainable and eco-friendly – The wood products in Tom's condos

shabby and loose-fitting – Marie's old gray sweater

rusty – Marie's high-school French

creative and competent – Ellen's training style

honest, decent and unpretentious – Mrs. Bertoli's sons

2

as smart and capable as; refused to spend; unlike Ellen; to be promoted; determined to; deserved

Not needed: advance her career; planned to impress

C Activities

Students' own answers